John Bunyan, Alexander Smith

Divine Emblems

John Bunyan, Alexander Smith

Divine Emblems

ISBN/EAN: 9783337780098

Printed in Europe, USA, Canada, Australia, Japan

Cover: Foto ©Lupo / pixelio.de

More available books at **www.hansebooks.com**

Divine Emblems,

OR,

TEMPORAL THINGS

SPIRITUALISED, &c.

WITH PREFACE BY ALEXANDER SMITH,
AUTHOR OF "DREAMTHORP,"

LONDON: BICKERS & SON.

John Bunyan

PREFACE.

By ALEXANDER SMITH,
AUTHOR OF "DREAMTHORP," ETC.

JOHN BUNYAN has written his biography in brief in the sentence which opens "The Pilgrim's Progreſs"—"As I walked through the wildernefs of this world, I lighted on a certain place where there was a den, and I laid me down in that place to sleep; and as I slept, I dreamed a dream." He dreamed his dream; he told it in the moſt childlike way; and now the world will as soon forget Shakſpeare as it will forget him. He is the prince of dreamers, as Homer is the prince of poets. The scenery of his viſion has become familiar as the scenery which surrounds our homes. We know the whole courfe of the journey—from the City of Deftruction to the Slough of Defpond; paft the Houfe of the Interpreter; up Hill Difficulty; the meeting of Chriftian with the Maidens, Piety, Prudence, and Charity; Chriftian's reft in the "large upper chamber whofe window opened toward the sun-rifing," the name of which chamber was Peace; the journey down into the Valley of the Shadow of Death: the combat which took place there; Vanity Fair and the burning of Faithful; the imprifonment of Hopeful and Chriftian by the Giant, and their efcape; the Delectable Mountains, with the Golden City seen in the diftance shining like a star; the Land of Beulah; the paffage acrofs the dark river, with troops of angels, and melody of hymns and trumpets, waiting the pilgrims on the further bank;—all this every boy knows as he knows the way to school—with this every man is familiar as with his perfonal experience—and the curious thing is, that the incidents and the scenery which we accept with such belief are but the dark conceits and shadows of things; in all there is more than meets the eye. Under everything lies the moft solemn meanings. "The Pilgrim's Progrefs" is not only the moft enchanting story in the world, it is one of the beft manuals of theology. The boy devours it as he does "Robinfon Crufoe;" the devout man values it next to his Bible. As a story, it is full of the moft charming, moft natural, sometimes moft terrible things. In the second part—which, compared with the firft, is as the

Odyſſey to the Iliad—what can be prettier than the boy sitting singing in the Valley of Humiliation with the herb *Heart's Eaſe* in his boſom? Read the fight between Chriſtian and Apollyon, and note the touch of imagination—"In this combat no man can imagine, unleſs he had seen and heard as I did, what yelling and hideous roaring Apollyon made all the time of the fight—he spake like a dragon; and, on the other side, what sighs and groans burſt from Chriſtian's heart. I never saw him all the while give so much as one pleaſant look, till he perceived he had wounded Apollyon with his two-edged sword; *then, indeed, he did smile and look upward;* but it was the dreadfulleſt sight I ever saw." And after the pilgrims have paſſed the river—"Juſt as the gates were opened to let in the men, I looked in after them, and, behold, the city shone like the sun; the streets alſo were paved with gold, and in them walked many men with crowns on their heads, palms in their hands, and golden harps to sing praiſes withal. There were alſo of them that had wings, and they anſwered one another without intermiſſion, saying, 'Holy, holy, holy is the Lord.' And after that they shut the gates, which, *when I had seen, I wiſhed myſelf among them.*" How *naive* this laſt confeſſion—the writer becoming enſlaved by his own sorcery. Lord Macaulay has pointed out, in a memorable eſſay, the reſemblance that exiſts between Bunyan and Spenſer— the one nurtured from his childhood on chivalric story, a high Platonist, the friend of Sir Philip Sydney; the other a Bedfordshire tinker, almost uneducated, addicted in his early days to dancing, bell-ringing, and the swearing of strange oaths, at last the wandering preacher of a despised sect. The men were curiously unlike in some respects, but in point of genius they had much in common. Both were of "imagination all compact." To each every object was a mirror in which he saw something else. Both delighted in intricate allegories. Spenser had more fancy, colour, music, and picturesqueness; Bunyan more homeliness, interest in common things, shrewdness, humour, and mother wit. Spenser is a good deal what Bunyan would have been had he come of a gentle stock in Elizabeth's reign, been educated at the universities, been the friend of the most chivalric spirit that ever trod English ground. Bunyan is a good deal what Spenser would have been had he lived a tinker, gone through the fierce spiritual experiences described in "Grace Abounding," settled finally into an itinerant Baptist preacher, and got a jail for twelve years to dream out his dream in. "The Fairy Queen" and "The Pilgrim's Progress" are the two greatest allegorical works in our language; and Bunyan has over Spenser one considerable advantage, in that, while no reader has been able to read through the poem, no reader before the close has been able to lay down the story.

Bunyan's ruling faculty was imagination, and he posfelfed it in perilous excefs. In his " Grace Abounding"—certainly one of the moft curious and striking of autobiographical sketches—we see how it domineered over him, and made him for a time a dweller on the shores of Tophet. It brought all his paft sins before him—his dancing, his bell-ringing, his Sabbath-breaking, his profane oaths—with more than their warranted terrors, and they difturbed his quiet as the ghoft of Banquo difturbed the quiet of Macbeth. And when contrition brought peace and a new mode of life, it created for him the Delectable Mountains peopled with amiable shepherds; it made blaze for him the Celeftial City, and made audible the melodious voices of its inhabitants. When he secured spiritual peace, his prevailing mood of mind became a certain devout fancifulnefs, and his long confinement—for he wrote the greater proportion of his books in prifon—made the exercife of this fancifulnefs a more than ordinary relief.

> "When the body is up-mew'd,
> Then the fancy furthest flies."

Bunyan dreamed his dream, and supported his own spirit; he made tagged thread-laces and supported his wife and family,—and so the years wore on. He was a profoundly religious man; but when his religion had become habitual and terrorlefs, he handed it over to Fancy, that she might play with it. And juft as the ancient pagan heard Pan's pipe in the thicket, saw the hamadryad issue from the tree "like mufic from an inftrument," caught in the fountain the momentary gleam of a naiad's limbs and face, he saw spiritual meanings in the afpects of external nature and in the ongoings of domeftic life; found something to pierce the confcience in the lark quivering in mid-air above its neft; and difcovered the illuftration of a doctrine in the pot simmering upon the cottage fire. In every material object he saw a spiritual similitude. He was a religious Æfop, with a fable for everything that might occur. "The Pilgrim's Progrefs" is a long similitude, but in its courfe it contains many minor similitudes—as, for inftance, in the objects shewn to Chriftian at the houfe of the Interpreter. This devout playfulnefs, with a conftant eye for the practical application; this sermonifing in difguife; this mafquerading with a serious brow beneath the vizor, which is sure to be shewn at the proper time, is a mood in which Bunyan loved to indulge, and in which he is almoft always succefsful. In the prefent little book of "Divine Emblems" he gives free rein to his fantafy; he finds texts in the moft unlikely places, and from thefe texts he extracts the moft unexpected sermons. He difplays art and ingenuity; and the meanings he deduces from the objects with which he works are for the moft part pertinent and natural. There is a further charm in the book, in that it is written in verfe. Bunyan's mufe is clad in ruffet, wears shoes and stockings, has a country accent, and walks along the level Bedfordfhire roads. If as a poet he is homely and idiomatic, he is always natural, straightforward, and sincere. His lines are unpoliſhed, but they have pith and sinew, like the talk of a shrewd peaſant. In the "Emblems" there are many touches of pure poetry, shewing that in his mind there was a vein of silver which, under favourable circumſtances, might have been worked to rich iſſues; and everywhere there is an admirable homely pregnancy and fulneſs of meaning. He has the strong thought, and the knack of the skilled workman to drive, by a single blow, the nail home to the head.

In his Addreſs to the Reader, Bunyan, in a mood somewhat satirical, explains his motive for taking the homelieſt objects and making them the emblems of divine things. He reſolved to come as if in play to a volatile generation, that he might catch attention. Men and women are but children, he says—

> "And since at gravity they make a tush,
> My very beard I cast behind a bush;
> And, like a fool, stand fingering of their toys,
> And all to shew they are but girls and boys."

And in defence of the "inconſiderableneſs of things" by which he expreſſes his mind, he defends himſelf in this wiſe—

> "I could, were I so pleased, use higher strains,
> And, for applause, on tenters strain my brains;
> But what needs that? the arrow out of sight,
> Does n t the sleeper nor the watchman fright.
> To shoot too high doth make but children gaze,
> 'Tis that which hits the man doth him amaze."

And he has fulfilled his purpofe, for not unfrequently he "hits" the very heart.

All men know "The Holy War" and "The Pilgrim's Progrefs," but the "Divine Emblems" have fallen out of human memory. This is a pity; and to the prefent publifhers it has seemed proper to produce a new edition, with all the quaint head and tail pieces of a unique edition long out of print, publifhed by W. Johnfton, Ludgate Hill, in 1767. The book is as suitable for boys and girls as it was two hundred years ago—and boys and girls are readers now, which they were not in Bunyan's day. To boys and girls of all ages the "Divine Emblems" may be commended. In truth, this little book is as in some sort a pantomime; but devout fancy is the wand which rules the scenes, and at its stroke into divine truths and weighty morals the commoneft objects are transformed.

TO THE READER.

OURTEOUS READER,

 The title-page will shew, if thou wilt look,
 What are the proper subjects of this book :
They 're boys and girls, of all sorts and degrees,
From those of age, to children on the knees.
Thus comprehensive am I in my notions,
They tempt me to it by their childish motions.
We now have boys with beards, and girls that be
Huge as old women, wanting gravity.
Then do not blame me, since I thus describe them,
Flatter I may not, lest thereby I bribe them

To have a better judgment of themselves,
Than wife men have of babies on the shelves.
Their antic tricks, fantaftic modes, and way,
Shew they like very boys and girls do play
With all the frantic fooleries of the age,
And that in open view, as on a stage;
Our bearded men do act like beardlefs boys,
Our women pleafe themfelves with childifh toys.
Our minifters long time by word and pen
Dealt with them, counting them not boys, but men:
They shot their thunders at them and their toys,
But hit them not, 'caufe they were girls and boys.
The better charged, the wider still they shot,
Or elfe so high, that dwarfs they touched not.
Inftead of men, they found them girls and boys,
To nought addicted but to childifh toys.

Wherefore, dear reader, that I save them may,
I now with them the very devil play.
And since at gravity they make a tufh,
My very beard I caft behind a bufh;
And, like a fool, stand fingering of their toys,
And all to shew they are but girls and boys.

Nor do I blufh, although I think some may
Call me a child, becaufe I with them play:

TO THE READER.

I aim to shew them how each fingle-fangle
On which they dote, does but their souls entangle,
As with a web, a trap, a gin, a snare,
And will deftroy them, have they not a care.

Paul seem'd to play the fool, that he might gain,
Thofe that are fools indeed, if not in grain;
He did it by such things to let them see
Their emptinefs, their sin and vanity;
A noble act, and full of honefty!
Nor he, nor I, would like them be in vice,
But by their playthings I would them entice,
That they might raife their thoughts from childifh toys
To heaven, for that's prepared for girls and boys.
Nor would I so confine myfelf to thefe,
As to shun graver things; but seek to pleafe
Thofe more compofed with better things than toys,
Though I would thus be catching girls and boys.

Wherefore if men inclined are to look,
Perhaps their graver fancies may be took
With what is here, though but in homely rhymes:
But he who pleafes all muft rife betimes.
Some, I perfuade me, will be finding fault,
Concluding, here I trip, and there I halt:
No doubt, some could thofe grovelling notions raife
By fine-fpun terms, that challenge might the bays.

Should all be forced their brains to lay afide,
That cannot regulate the flowing tide
By this or that man's fancy, we should have
The wife unto the fool become a slave.
What though my text seems mean, my morals be
Grave, as if fetch'd from a sublimer tree.
And if some better handle can a fly
Than some a text, wherefore should we deny
Their making proof, or good experiment,
Of smalleft things great mischiefs to prevent?

Wife Solomon did fools to pifmires send
To learn true wifdom, and their lives to mend.
Yea, God by swallows, cuckoos, and the afs,
Shews they are fools who let that seafon pafs,
Which He put in their hand, that to obtain
Which is both prefent and eternal gain.

I think the wifer sort my rhyme may slight,
While I perufe them, fools will take delight.
Then what care I? the foolifh, God has chofe;
And doth by foolifh things their minds compofe,
And settle upon that which is divine;
Great things by little ones are made to shine.

I could, were I so pleafed, use higher strains,
And, for applaufe, on tenters strain my brains;

TO THE READER.

But what needs that? the arrow out of sight,
Does not the sleeper nor the watchman fright.
To shoot too high doth make but children gaze,
'Tis that which hits the man doth him amaze.

As for the inconfiderablenefs
Of things, by which I do my mind exprefs,
May I by them bring some good things to pafs,
As Samfon with the jaw-bone of an afs,
Or as brave Shamgar with his ox's goad,
(Both things unmanly, not for war in mode,)
I have my end, though I myfelf expofe,
For God will have the glory at the clofe.

J. B.

CONTENTS.

		PAGE
I.	UPON THE BARREN FIG-TREE IN GOD'S VINEYARD,	3
II.	UPON THE LARK AND THE FOWLER,	5
III.	UPON THE VINE-TREE,	8
IV.	MEDITATIONS UPON AN EGG,	10
V.	OF FOWLS FLYING IN THE AIR,	12
VI.	UPON THE LORD'S PRAYER,	14
VII.	MEDITATIONS UPON THE PEEP OF DAY,	15
VIII.	UPON THE FLINT IN THE WATER,	16
IX.	UPON THE FISH IN THE WATER,	18

CONTENTS.

	PAGE
X. UPON THE SWALLOW,	20
XI. UPON THE BEE,	21
XII. UPON A LOW'RING MORNING,	22
XIII. UPON OVER-MUCH NICENESS,	24
XIV. MEDITATIONS UPON A CANDLE,	26
XV. UPON THE SACRAMENTS,	30
XVI. UPON THE SUN'S REFLECTION UPON THE CLOUDS IN A FAIR MORNING,	31
XVII. UPON APPAREL,	32
XVIII. THE SINNER AND THE SPIDER,	33
XIX. MEDITATIONS UPON THE DAY BEFORE THE SUN-RISING,	43
XX. OF THE MOLE IN THE GROUND,	44
XXI. OF THE CUCKOO,	46
XXII. OF THE BOY AND BUTTERFLY,	48
XXIII. OF THE FLY AT THE CANDLE,	50
XXIV. ON THE RISING OF THE SUN,	52
XXV. UPON THE PROMISING FRUITFULNESS OF A TREE,	54

CONTENTS. xxi

		PAGE
XXVI.	UPON THE THIEF,	56
XXVII.	OF THE CHILD WITH THE BIRD ON THE BUSH,	59
XXVIII.	OF MOSES AND HIS WIFE,	63
XXIX.	OF THE ROSE-BUSH,	65
XXX.	OF THE GOING DOWN OF THE SUN,	67
XXXI.	UPON THE FROG,	69
XXXII.	UPON THE WHIPPING OF A TOP,	71
XXXIII.	UPON THE PISMIRE,	72
XXXIV.	UPON THE BEGGAR,	73
XXXV.	UPON THE HORSE AND HIS RIDER,	75
XXXVI.	UPON THE SIGHT OF A POUND OF CANDLES FALLING TO THE GROUND,	78
XXXVII.	UPON A PENNY LOAF,	80
XXXVIII.	THE BOY AND WATCHMAKER,	81
XXXIX.	UPON A LOOKING-GLASS.	83
XL.	OF THE LOVE OF CHRIST,	85
XLI.	ON THE CACKLING OF A HEN,	88
XLII.	UPON AN HOUR-GLASS,	89

CONTENTS.

		PAGE
XLIII.	UPON A SNAIL,	90
XLIV.	OF THE SPOUSE OF CHRIST,	92
XLV.	UPON A SKILFUL PLAYER ON AN INSTRUMENT,	95
XLVI.	OF MAN BY NATURE,	97
XLVII.	UPON THE DISOBEDIENT CHILD,	98
XLVIII.	UPON A SHEET OF WHITE PAPER,	101
XLIX.	UPON THE FIRE,	103

Divine Emblems;

OR,

TEMPORAL THINGS SPIRITUALISED, &c

A

I.

UPON THE BARREN FIG-TREE IN GOD'S VINEYARD.

HAT barren here! in this so good a soil?
The sight of this doth make God's heart recoil
From giving thee his blessing; barren tree,
Bear fruit, or else thy end will cursed be!

Art thou not planted by the water-side?
Know'st not thy Lord by fruit is glorified?
The sentence is, Cut down the barren tree:
Bear fruit, or else thy end will cursed be!

Thou haſt been digg'd about and dunged too,
Will neither patience, nor yet dreſſing do?
The executioner is come, O tree,
Bear fruit, or elſe thine end will curſed be!

He that about thy root takes pains to dig,
Would, if on thee were found but one good fig,
Preſerve thee from the axe: but, barren tree,
Bear fruit, or elſe thy end will curſed be!

The utmoſt end of patience is at hand,
'Tis much if thou much longer here doth stand.
O cumber-ground, thou art a barren tree,
Bear fruit, or elſe thy end will curſed be!

Thy standing, nor thy name, will help at all;
When fruitful trees are spared, thou muſt fall.
The axe is laid unto thy roots, O tree,
Bear fruit, or elſe thy end will curſed be!

II.

UPON THE LARK AND THE FOWLER.

THOU simple bird, what makes thee here to play?
Look, there's the fowler, pr'ythee come away.
Doſt not behold the net? Look there 'tis spread,
Venture a little further, thou art dead.

Is there not room enough in all the field,
For thee to play in, but thou needs muſt yield
To the deceitful glitt'ring of a glaſs,
Between nets placed, to bring thy death to paſs?

Bird, if thou art so much for dazzling light,
Look, there's the sun above thee, dart upright
Thy nature is to soar up to the sky,
Why wilt thou then come down to the nets and die?

Heed not the fowler's tempting flatt'ring call;
This whiftle he enchanteth birds withal:
What though thou see'ft a live bird in his net.
She's there, becaufe from thence she cannot get.

Look how he tempteth thee with his decoy,
That he may rob thee of thy life, thy joy,
Come, pr'ythee bird, I pr'ythee come away,
Why shouldft thou to this net become a prey?

Hadft thou not wings, or were thy feathers pull'd,
Or waft thou blind, or faft afleep wert lull'd:
The cafe would somewhat alter, but for thee,
Thy eyes are ope', and thou haft wings to flee.

Remember that thy song is in thy rise,
Not in thy fall: earth's not thy paradife.
Keep up aloft then, let thy circuits be
Above, where birds from fowlers' nets are free.

FOR YOUTH.

COMPARISON.

This fowler is an emblem of the devil,
His nets and whiftle, figures of all evil.
His glafs an emblem is of sinful pleafure,
Decoying such, who reckon sin a treafure.

The simple lark's a shadow of a saint,
Under allurings, ready now to faint.
What you have read, a needful warning is,
Design'd to shew the soul its share of blifs,
And how it may this fowler's net efcape,
And not commit upon itfelf this rape.

III.

UPON THE VINE-TREE.

WHAT is the vine more than another tree?
Nay moſt, than it, more tall, more comely be:
What workman thence will take a beam or pin,
To make out which may be delighted in?
Its excellency in its fruit doth lie:
A fruitleſs vine, it is not worth a fly.

COMPARISON.

What are profeſſors more than other men?
Nothing at all. Nay, there's not one in ten,

Either for wealth, or wit, that may compare
In many things, with some that carnal are.
Good then they are, when mortified their sin :
But without that, they are not worth a pin.

IV.

MEDITATIONS UPON AN EGG.

HE egg's no chick by falling from the hen;
Nor man a Chriftian till he's born again.

The egg's at firft contained in the shell:
Men, afore grace, in sins and darknefs dwell.
The egg, when laid, by warmth is made a chicken,
And Chrift by grace the dead in sin does quicken.
The chick at firft is in the shell confined;
So heav'n-born souls are in the flefh detain'd.
The shell doth crack, the chick doth chirp and peep,
The flefh decays, and men then pray and weep.

The shell doth break, the chick's at liberty,
The flesh falls off, the soul mounts up on high.
But both do not enjoy the self-same plight;
The soul is safe, the chick now fears the kite.

But chicks from rotten eggs do not proceed;
Nor is a hypocrite a saint indeed.
The rotten egg, though underneath the hen,
If crack'd, stinks, and is loathsome unto men.
Nor doth her warmth make what is rotten sound;
What's rotten, rotten will at laſt be found.
The hypocrite, sin has him in poſſeſſion,
He is a rotten egg under profeſſion.

Some eggs bring cockatrices; and some men
Some hatch'd and brooded in the viper's den.
Some eggs bring wild-fowls; and some men there be
As wild as are the wildeſt fowls that flee.
Some eggs bring spiders; and some men appear
More venom'd than the worſt of spiders are.
Some eggs bring piſmires; and some seem to me
As much for trifles as the piſmires be.
And thus do divers eggs from diff'rent shapes,
As like some men as monkeys are like apes.
But this is but an egg, were it a chick,
Here had been legs, and wings, and bones to pick.

V.

OF FOWLS FLYING IN THE AIR.

METHINKS I see a sight moſt excellent,
All sorts of birds fly in the firmament:
Some great, some small, all of a divers kind,
Mine eye affecting, pleaſant to my mind.
Look how they wing along the wholeſome air,
Above the world of worldlings, and their care.
And as they divers are in bulk and hue,
So are they in their way of flying too.
So many birds, so many various things
Swim in the element upon their wings.

COMPARISON.

These birds are emblems of those men, that shall
Ere long possess the heavens, their all in all.
They each are of a diff'rent shape and kind ;
To teach, we of all nations there shall find.
They are some great, some little as we see,
To shew some great, some small in glory be.
Their flying diversely, as we behold,
Do shew saints' joys will there be manifold.
Some glide, some mount, some flutter, and some do,
In a mix'd way of flying, glory too.
To shew that each shall to his full content,
Be happy in that heav'nly firmament.

VI.

UPON THE LORD'S PRAYER.

OUR Father which in heaven art,
    Thy name be always hallowed;
    Thy kingdom come, thy will be done;
Thy heavenly path be followed:
    By us on earth, as 'tis with thee,
      We humbly pray;
    And let our bread to us be giv'n
      From day to day.
Forgive our debts, as we forgive
    Thofe that to us indebted are:
Into temptation lead us not;
    But save us from the wicked snare.
    The kingdom's thine, the power too,
      We thee adore;
    The glory alfo shall be thine
      For evermore.

VII.

MEDITATIONS UPON THE PEEP OF DAY.

AT peep of day I often cannot know
Whether 'tis night, whether 'tis day or no.
I fancy that I see a little light,
But cannot yet diftinguifh day from night;
I hope, I doubt, but certain yet I be not,
I am not at a point, the sun I see not.
Thus such, who are but juft of grace poffeft,
They know not yet if they be curft or bleft.

VIII.

UPON THE FLINT IN THE WATER.

HIS flint, time out of mind has there abode,
Where chryftal streams make their continual road;
Yet it abides a flint as much as 'twere,
Before it touch'd the water or came there.

Its hardnefs is not in the leaft abated,
'Tis not at all by water penetrated.
Though water hath a soft'ning virtue in 't,
It can't diffolve the stone, for 'tis a flint.

Yea, though in the water it doth still remain,
Its fiery nature still it does retain.
If you oppofe it with its oppofite,
Then in your very face its fire 'twill spit.

COMPARISON.

This flint an emblem is of thofe that lie,
Under the word like stones, until they die.
Its cryftal streams have not their natures changed,
They are not from their lufts by grace eftranged.

IX.

UPON THE FISH IN THE WATER.

HE water is the fiſh's element:
Take her from thence, none can her death prevent,
And some have said, who have tranſgreſſors been,
As good not be, as to be kept from sin.

The water is the fiſh's element:
Leave her but there, and she is well content.
So 's he, who in the path of life doth plod,
Take all, says he, let me but have my God.

The water is the fish's element:
Her sportings there to her are excellent:
So is God's service unto holy men,
They are not in their element till then.

X.

UPON THE SWALLOW.

THIS pretty bird, oh! how she flies and sings!
But could she do so if she had not wings?
Her wings befpeak my faith, her songs my peace;
When I believe and sing, my doubtings ceafe.

XI.

UPON THE BEE.

THE bee goes out, and honey home doth bring;
And some who seek that honey find a sting!
Now wouldſt thou have the honey, and be free
From stinging; in the firſt place kill the bee.

COMPARISON.

This bee an emblem truly is of sin,
Whoſe sweet unto a many, death has been.
Wouldſt thou have sweet from sin, and yet not die,
Sin in the firſt place thou muſt mortify.

XII.

UPON A LOWERING MORNING.

WELL, with the day I see the clouds appear;
 And mix the light with darkneſs ev'rywhere;
 This threatens thoſe who on long journeys go,
That they shall meet the slabby rain or snow.
Elſe while I gaze, the sun doth with his beams
Belace the clouds, as 'twere with bloody streams;
Then suddenly thoſe clouds do wat'ry grow,
And weep and pour their tears out where they go.

COMPARISON.

Thus 'tis when gospel light doth usher in
To us, both sense of grace and sense of sin;
Yea, when it makes sin red with Jesus' blood,
Then we can weep till weeping does us good.

XIII.

UPON OVER-MUCH NICENESS.

IS strange to see how over-nice are some
    About their clothes, their bodies, and their
        home:
While what's of worth, they slightly pafs it by,
Not doing it at all, or slovenly.

Their houfes muft well furnifh'd be in print;
While their immortal soul has no good in 't.
Its outfide alfo they muft beautify,
While there is in 't scarce common honefty.

Their bodies they muft have trick'd up and trim :
Their infide full of filth up to the brim.
Upon their clothes there muft not be a spot,
Whereas their lives are but one common blot.

How nice, how coy are some about their diet,
That can their crying souls with hog's-meat quiet.
All muft be dreft t' a hair, or elfe 'tis naught,
While of the living bread they have no thought.
Thus for their outfide they are clean and nice,
While their poor infide stinks with sin and vice.

XIV.

MEDITATIONS UPON A CANDLE.

MAN 'S like a candle in a candleſtick,
Made up of tallow and a little wick;
For what the candle is, before 'tis lighted,
Juſt such be they who are in sin benighted.
Nor can a man his soul with grace inſpire,
More than the candles set themſelves on fire.

Candles receive their light from what they are not;
Men grace from Him, for whom at firſt they care not.
We manage candles when they take the fire;
God men, when He with grace doth them inſpire.

And biggeſt candles give the better light,
As grace on biggeſt sinners shines moſt bright.
The candle shines to make another see,
A saint unto his neighbour light should be.
The blinking candle we do much deſpiſe,
Saints dim of light are high in no man's eyes.

Again, though it may seem to some a riddle,
We uſe to light our candle at the middle:
True light doth at a candle's end appear,
And grace the heart firſt reaches by the ear;
But 'tis the wick the fire doth kindle on,
As 'tis the heart that grace firſt works upon.
Thus both to faſten upon what's the main,
And so their life and vigour do maintain.

The tallow makes the wick yield to the fire,
And sinful fleſh doth make the soul deſire
That grace may kindle on it, in it burn;
So evil makes the soul from evil turn.

But candles in the wind are apt to flare,
And Chriſtians in a tempeſt to deſpair.
We see the flame with smoke attended is;
And in our holy lives there's much amiſs.

Sometimes a thief will candle-light annoy:
And luſts do seek our graces to deſtroy.

What brackiſh is will make a candle sputter;
'Twixt sin and grace there's oft a heavy clutter.
Sometimes the light burns dim, 'cauſe of the snuff,
And sometimes 'tis blown quite out with a puff:
But watchfulneſs preventeth both theſe evils,
Keeps candles light, and grace in spite of devils.

But let not snuffs nor puffs make us to doubt;
Our candles may be lighted, though puff'd out.
The candle in the night doth all excel,
Nor sun, nor moon, nor stars, then shine so well,
So is the Chriſtian in our hemiſphere,
Whoſe light shews others how their courſe to steer.
When candles are put out, all's in confuſion;
Where Chriſtians are not, devils make intruſion.
They then are happy who such candles have,
All others dwell in darkneſs and the grave.
But candles that do blink within the socket,
And saints whoſe eyes are always in their pocket,
Are much alike; such candles make us fumble;
And at such saints, good men and bad do stumble.

Good candles don't offend, except sore eyes,
Nor hurt, unleſs it be the silly flies:
Thus none like burning candles in the night,
Nor ought to holy living for delight.
But let us draw towards the candle's end:
The fire, you see, doth wick and tallow spend;

As grace man's life, until his glafs is run,
And so the candle and the man is done.

The man now lays him down upon his bed;
The wick yields up its fire; and so is dead.
The candle now extinct is, but the man,
By grace mounts up to glory, there to stand.

XV.

UPON THE SACRAMENTS

WO sacraments I do believe there be,
    Even baptifm and the supper of the Lord;
   Both myfteries divine, which do to me,
By God's appointment, benefit afford:
But shall they be my God, or shall I have
   Of them so foul and impious a thought,
To think that from the curfe they can me save?
   Bread, wine, nor water me no ranfom bought.

XVI.

UPON THE SUN'S REFLECTION UPON THE CLOUDS IN A FAIR MORNING.

LOOK yonder, ah! methinks mine eyes do see
Clouds edged with silver, as fine garments be!
They look as if they saw the golden face
That makes black clouds moſt beautiful with grace.
Unto the saints sweet incenſe of their prayer,
Theſe smoky curl'd clouds I do compare.
For as theſe clouds seem edged, or laced with gold,
Their prayers return with bleſſings manifold.

XVII.

UPON APPAREL.

GOD gave us clothes to hide our nakedneſs,
    And we by them do it expoſe to view;
Our pride and unclean minds, to an exceſs,
    By our apparel we to others shew.

XVIII.

THE SINNER AND THE SPIDER.

SINNER.

HAT black, what ugly crawling thing art thou?

SPIDER.

I am a spider ——————

SINNER.

A spider, ay; truly a filthy creature.

SPIDER.

Not filthy as thyself in name or feature:

My name entailed is to my creation;
My features, from the God of thy salvation.

SINNER.

I am a man, and in God's image made,
I have a soul shall neither die nor fade:
God has poffeffed me with human reafon,
Speak not againft me, left thou speakeft treafon;
For if I am the image of my Maker,
Of slander laid on me He is partaker.

SPIDER.

I know thou art a creature far above me,
Therefore I shun, I fear, and alfo love thee.
But though thy God hath made thee such a creature,
Thou haft againft Him often play'd the traitor.
Thy sin has fetch'd thee down: leave off to boaft;
Nature thou haft defiled, God's image loft,
Yea, thou thyfelf a very beaft haft made,
And art become like grafs, which soon doth fade.
Thy soul, thy reafon, yea, thy spotlefs state,
Sin has subjected to th' moft dreadful fate.
But I retain my primitive condition,
I 've all but what I loft by thy ambition.

SINNER.

Thou venom'd thing, I know not what to call thee;
The dregs of nature surely did befall thee;

Thou waſt compoſed o' th' droſs and scum of all,
Men hate thee, and, in scorn, thee *Spider* call.

SPIDER.

My venom's good for something, since God made it;
Thy nature sin hath spoil'd, and doth degrade it.
Thou art deſpoil'd of good: and though I fear thee,
I will not, though I might, deſpiſe and jeer thee.
Thou say'ſt I am the very dregs of nature,
Thy sin's the spawn of devils, 'tis no creature.
Thou say'ſt man hates me, 'cauſe I am a spider.
Poor man, thou at thy God art a derider;
My venom tendeth to my preſervation;
Thy pleaſing follies work out thy damnation.
Poor man, I keep the rules of my creation,
Thy sin has caſt thee headlong from thy station.
I hurt nobody willingly; but thou
Art a self-murderer: thou know'ſt not how
To do what's good; no, for thou loveſt evil:
Thou fly'ſt God's law, adhereſt to the devil.

SINNER.

Thou ill-shaped thing, there's an antipathy
'Twixt man and spiders, 'tis in vain to lie;
Stand off, I hate thee—if thou doſt come nigh me,
I'll cruſh thee with my foot; I do defy thee.

SPIDER.

They are ill-shaped who warped are by sin,
Hatred in thee to God hath long time been;
No marvel then indeed, if me, His creature,
Thou doft defy, pretending name and feature.
But why stand off? My presence shall not throng thee,
'Tis not my venom, but thy sin doth wrong thee.

Come, I will teach thee wisdom, do but hear me,
I was made for thy profit, do not fear me.
But if thy God thou wilt not hearken to,
What can the swallow, ant, and spider do?
Yet I will speak, I can but be rejected,
Sometimes great things by small means are effected.

Hark, then, though man is noble by creation,
He's lapfed now to such degeneration
As not to grieve, so carelefs he is grown,
Though he himfelf has sadly overthrown,
And brought to bondage every earthly thing,
Ev'n from the very spider to the king:
This we poor senfitives do feel and see;
For subject to the curfe you made us be.
Tread not upon me, neither from me go;
'Tis man who has brought all the world to woe.

The law of my creation bids me teach thee;
I will not for thy pride to God impeach thee.

I spin, I weave, and all to let thee see
Thy beft performances but cobwebs be.
Thy glory now is brought to such an ebb,
It doth not much excel the spider's web.
My webs becoming snares and traps for flies,
Do set the wiles of hell before thine eyes;
Their tangling nature is to let thee see
Thy sins, too, of a tangling nature be;
My den, or hole, for that 'tis bottomlefs,
Doth of damnation shew the lastingnefs.
My lying quiet till the fly is catch'd,
Shews secretly hell hath thy ruin hatch'd.
In that I on her seize, when she is taken,
I shew who gathers, whom God hath forfaken.
The fly lies buzzing in my web, to tell
How finners always roar and howl in hell.

Now fince I shew thee all thefe myfteries,
How canft thou hate me, or me scandalife?

SINNER.

Well, well, I will no more be a derider,
I did not look for such things from a spider.

SPIDER.

Come, hold thy peace, what I have yet to say,
If heeded, may help thee another day.
Since I an ugly ven'mous creature be,
There's some refemblance 'twixt vile man and me.

My wild and heedless runnings are like those
Whose ways to ruin do their souls expose.
Daylight is not my time, I work i' th' night,
To shew they are like me who hate the light.
The maid sweeps one web down, I make another,
To shew how heedless ones convictions smother.
My web is no defence at all to me,
Nor will false hopes at judgment be to thee.

SINNER.

O spider, I have heard thee, and do wonder
A spider should thus lighten and thus thunder!

SPIDER.

Do but hold still, and I will let thee see,
Yet in my ways more mysteries there be.
Shall not I do thee good, if I thee tell,
I shew to thee a four-fold way to hell?
For since I set my web in sundry places,
I shew men go to hell in divers traces.

One I set in the window, that I might
Shew some go down to hell with gospel-light.
One I set in a corner, as you see,
To shew how some in secret snared be.
Gross webs great store I set in darksome places,
To shew how many sin with brazen faces.
Another web I set aloft on high,
To shew there's some professing men must die.

Thus in my ways, God's wifdom doth conceal;
And by my ways that wifdom doth reveal.

I hide myself when I for flies do wait,
So doth the devil when he lays his bait;
If I do fear the lofing of my prey,
I stir me, and more snares upon her lay.
This way, and that, her wings and legs I tie,
That sure as she is catch'd, so she muft die.
But if I see she's like to get away,
Then with my venom I her journey stay.
All which my ways the devil imitates,
To catch men, 'caufe he their salvation hates.

SINNER.

O spider, thou delight'ft me with thy skill,
I pr'ythee spit this venom at me still.

SPIDER.

I am a spider, yet I can poffefs
The palace of a king, where happinefs
So much abounds. Nor when I do go thither,
Do they afk what, or whence I come, or whither
I make my hafty travels; no, not they:
They let me pafs, and I go on my way.
I seize the palace, do with hands take hold
Of doors, of locks, or bolts; yet I am bold,
When in, to clamber up unto the throne,
And to poffefs it, as if 'twere my own.

Nor is there any law forbidding me
Here to abide, or in this palace be.

At pleasure I ascend the highest stories,
And there I sit, and so behold the glories
Myself is compass'd with, as if I were
One of the chiefest courtiers that be there.

Here lords and ladies do come round about me,
With grave demeanour, nor do any flout me
For this my brave adventure, no, not they;
They come, they go, but leave me there to stay.

Now, my reproacher, I do by all this
Shew how thou mayst possess thyself of bliss:
Thou art worse than a spider, but take hold
On Christ the door, thou shalt not be controll'd:
By Him do thou the heavenly palace enter;
None e'er will chide thee for thy brave adventure.
Approach thou then unto the very throne,
There speak thy mind; fear not, the day's thine
    own.
Nor saint, nor angel, will thee stop or stay,
But rather tumble blocks out of the way.
My venom stops not me; let not thy vice
Stop thee; possess thyself of paradise.

Go on, I say, although thou be a sinner,
Learn to be bold in faith, of me a spinner.

This is the way true glories to poſſeſs,
And to enjoy what no man can expreſs.

Sometimes I find the palace-door up-lock'd,
And so my entrance thither has up-block'd.
But am I daunted? No, I here and there
Do feel, and search; and so if anywhere,
At any chink or crevice find my way,
I crowd, I preſs for paſſage, make no stay:
And so through difficulty I attain
The palace, yea, the throne, where princes reign.
I crowd sometimes, as if I 'd burſt in sunder;
And art thou cruſh'd with striving, do not wonder.
Some scarce get in, and yet indeed they enter:
Knock, for they nothing have that nothing
    venture.

Nor will the king himſelf throw dirt on thee,
As thou haſt caſt reproaches upon me.
He will not hate thee, O thou foul backslider!
As thou didſt me, becauſe I am a spider.
Now, to conclude: since I much doctrine bring,
Slight me no more, call me not ugly thing;
God wiſdom hath unto the piſmire given,
And spiders may teach men the way to heaven.

SINNER.

Well, my good spider, I my errors see,
I was a fool for railing so at thee.

Thy nature, venom, and thy fearful hue,
But shew what sinners are, and what they do.
Thy way and works do alſo darkly tell
How some men go to heaven, and some to hell.
Thou art my monitor, I am a fool;
They may learn, that to spiders go to school.

XIX.

MEDITATIONS UPON THE DAY BEFORE THE SUN-RISING.

BUT all this while, where's he whofe golden rays
Drives night away, and beautifies our days?
Where's he whofe goodly face doth warm and heal,
And shew us what the darkfome nights conceal?
Where's he that thaws our ice, drives cold away?
Let's have him, or we care not for the day.

Thus 'tis with thofe who are poffeff'd of grace,
There's nought to them like their Redeemer's face.

XX.

OF THE MOLE IN THE GROUND.

HE Mole's a creature very smooth and slick,
    She digs i' th' dirt, but 'twill not on her stick.
    So 's he who counts this world his greateſt
        gains,
Yet nothing gets but labour for his pains.
Earth 's the Mole's element, she can't abide
To be above ground, dirt-heaps are her pride;
And he is like her, who the worldling plays,
He imitates her in her works and ways.

Poor silly Mole, that thou shouldſt love to be
Where thou, nor sun, nor moon, nor stars canſt see.
But oh! how silly's he, who doth not care
So he gets earth, to have of heaven a share!

XXI.

OF THE CUCKOO.

THOU booby, say'ft thou nothing but Cuckoo?
The Robin and the Wren can thee out-do.
They to us play through their little throats,
Not one, but sundry pretty tuneful notes.
But thou haft fellows, some like thee can do
Little but suck our eggs, and sing Cuckoo.

Thy notes do not firft welcome in our spring,
Nor doft its firft tokens to us bring.
Birds less than thee by far, like prophets, do
Tell us 'tis coming, though not by Cuckoo.

Nor doft thou summer have away with thee,
Though thou a yawling, bawling Cuckoo be.
When thou doft ceafe among us to appear,
Then doth our harveft bravely crown our year.
But thou haft fellows, some like thee can do
Little but suck our eggs, and sing Cuckoo.

Since Cuckoos forward not our early spring,
Nor help with notes to bring our harveft in :
And since, while here, she only makes a noife,
So pleafing unto none as girls and boys.
The Formalift we may compare her to,
For he doth suck our eggs, and sing Cuckoo.

XXII.

OF THE BOY AND BUTTERFLY.

BEHOLD, how eager this our little boy
   Is for a butterfly, as if all joy,
   All profits, honours, yea, and lasting pleasures,
Were wrapt up in her, or the richest treasures
Found in her would be bundled up together,
When all her all is lighter than a feather.

He halloos, runs, and cries out, Here, boys, here!
Nor doth he brambles or the nettles fear:
He stumbles at the mole-hills, up he gets,
And runs again, as one bereft of wits;

And all his labour and his large outcry
Is only for a silly butterfly.

COMPARISON.

This little boy an emblem is of thofe
Whofe hearts are wholly at the world's difpofe.
The butterfly doth reprefent to me
The world's beft things at beft but fading be.
All are but painted nothings and falfe joys,
Like this poor butterfly to thefe our boys.
His running through nettles, thorns, and briers,
To gratify his boyifh fond defires,
His tumbling over mole-hills to attain
His end, namely, his butterfly to gain;
Doth plainly shew what hazards some men run
To get what will be loft as soon as won.
Men seem in choice, than children far more wife,
Becaufe they run not after butterflies:
When yet, alas! for what are empty toys,
They follow children, like to beardlefs boys.

XXIII.

OF THE FLY AT THE CANDLE.

WHAT ails this fly, thus defperately to enter
A combat with the candle? Will she venture
To catch at light? Away, thou silly fly;
Thus doing, thou wilt burn thy wings and die.

But 'tis a folly her advice to give,
She'll kill the candle, or she will not live.
Slap, says she, at it; then she makes retreat,
So wheels about, and doth her blows repeat.

Nor doth the candle let her quite efcape,
But gives some little check unto the ape;
Throws up her nimble heels, and down she falls,
Where she lies sprawling, and for succour calls.

When she recovers, up she gets again,
And at the candle comes with might and main.
But now behold, the candle takes the fly,
And holds her, till she doth by burning die.

COMPARISON.

This candle is an emblem of that light
Our gofpel gives in this our darksome night.
The fly a lively picture is of those
That hate, and do this gofpel-light oppofe.
At laft the gofpel doth become their snare,
Doth them with burning hands in pieces tear.

XXIV.

ON THE RISING OF THE SUN.

LOOK, look, brave Sol doth peep up from beneath,
Shews us his golden face, doth on us breathe;
Yea, he doth compafs us around with glories,
Whilft he afcends up to his higheft stories.
Where he his banner over us difplays,
And gives us light to see our works and ways.

Nor are we now as at the peep of light,
To queftion, is it day, or is it night?

The night is gone, the shadow's fled away,
And now we are moſt certain that 'tis day.

And thus it is when Jesus shews His face,
And doth assure us of His love and grace.

XXV.

UPON THE PROMISING FRUITFULNESS OF A TREE.

 COMELY sight indeed it is to see
A world of bloffoms on an apple-tree:
Yet far more comely would this tree appear,
If all its dainty blooms young apples were.
But how much more might one upon it see,
If all would hang there till they ripe should be.
But moſt of all in beauty 'twould abound,
If every one should then be truly sound.
But we, alas! do commonly behold
Blooms fall apace, if mornings be but cold;

They, too, which hang till they young apples are,
By blafting winds, and vermin take defpair;
Store that do hang, while almoft ripe we see
By bluft'ring winds are shaken from the tree.
So that of many only some there be
That grow and thrive to full maturity.

COMPARISON.

This tree a perfect emblem is of thofe
Who do the garden of the Lord compofe.
Its blafted blooms are motions unto good,
Which chill affections do nip in the bud.

Thofe little apples which yet blafted are,
Shew some good purpofes no good fruits bear.
Thofe spoil'd by vermin are to let us see
How good attempts by bad thoughts ruin'd be.

Thofe which the wind blows down while they are green,
Shew good works have by trials spoiled been.
Thofe that abide, while ripe upon the tree,
Shew in a good man some ripe fruit will be.

Behold, then, how abortive some fruits are,
Which at the firft moft promifing doth appear.
The froft, the wind, the worm, with time doth shew,
There flow from much appearance works but few.

XXVI.

UPON THE THIEF.

THE thief when he doth steal thinks he doth gain;
Yet then the greateſt loſs he doth suſtain.
Come, thief, tell me thy gain, but do not falter,
When summ'd, what comes it to more than the halter?

Perhaps, thou 'lt say, The halter I defy;
So thou mayſt say, yet by the halter die.
Thou 'lt say, Then there 's an end; no, pr'ythee, hold,
He was no friend of thine that thee so told.

Hear thou the word of God, that will thee tell,
Without repentance, thieves muſt go to hell.
But should it be as thy falſe prophet says,
Yet naught but loſs doth come by thieviſh ways.

All honeſt men will flee thy company,
Thou liv'ſt a rogue, and so a rogue will die.
Innocent boldneſs thou haſt none at all,
Thy inward thoughts do thee a villain call.

Sometimes when thou ly'ſt warmly on thy bed
Thou art like one unto the gallows led.
Fear, as a conſtable, breaks in upon thee—
Thou art as if the town were up to stone thee.

If hogs do grunt, or silly rats do ruſtle,
Thou art in conſternation, think'ſt a buſtle
By men about the door is made to take thee:
And all becauſe good conſcience doth forſake thee.

Thy case is so deplorable and bad,
Thou shun'ſt to think on't, leſt thou shouldſt be mad:
Thou art beſet with mischiefs every way.
The gallows groaneth for thee every day.

Wherefore, I pr'ythee, thief, thy theft forbear,
Conſult thy safety, pr'ythee, have a care.
If once thy head be got within the nooſe,
'Twill be too late a longer life to chooſe.

As to the penitent thou readeſt of,
What's that to them who at repentance scoff.
Nor is that grace at thy command or pow'r,
That thou shouldſt put it off till the laſt hour.
I·pr'ythee, thief, think on't, and turn betime:
Few go to life who do the gallows climb.

XXVII.

OF THE CHILD WITH THE BIRD ON THE BUSH.

Y little bird, how canſt thou sit
    And sing amidſt so many thorns?
Let me but hold upon thee get,
    My love with honour thee adorns.

Thou art at preſent little worth;
    Five farthings none will give for thee.
But, pr'ythee, little bird, come forth,
    Thou of more value art to me.

'Tis true it is sunſhine to-day,
  To-morrow birds will have a storm ;
My pretty one, come thou away,
  My bosom then shall keep thee warm.

Thou subject art to cold o' nights,
  When darkneſs is thy covering ;
By day thy danger's great by kites,
  How canſt thou then sit there and sing?

Thy food is scarce and scanty too,
  'Tis worms and traſh which thou doſt eat ;
Thy preſent state I pity do,
  Come, I 'll provide thee better meat.

I 'll feed thee with white bread and milk,
  And sugar-plums, if thou them crave ;
I 'll cover thee with fineſt silk,
  That from the cold I may thee save.

My father's palace shall be thine,
  Yea, in it thou shalt sit and sing ;
My little bird, if thou 'lt be mine,
  The whole year round should be thy spring.

I 'll teach thee all the notes at court ;
  Unthought of music thou shalt play :
And all that thither do reſort
  Shall praiſe thee for it every day.

I'll keep thee safe from cat and cur,
  No manner o' harm shall come to thee:
Yea, I will be thy succourer,
  My bosom shall thy cabin be.

But lo, behold, the bird is gone;
  These charmings would not make her yield:
The child's left at the bush alone,
  The bird flies yonder o'er the field.

COMPARISON.

This child of Christ an emblem is;
  This bird to sinners I compare:
The thorns are like those sins of his
  Which do surround him everywhere.

Her songs, her food, and sunshine day,
  Are emblems of those foolish toys
Which to destruction lead the way,
  The fruit of worldly, empty joys.

The arguments this child doth choose
  To draw to him a bird thus wild,
Shews Christ familiar speech doth use
  To make him to be reconciled.

The bird, in that she takes her wing
  To speed her from Him after all,
Shews us vain man loves anything
  Much better than the heavenly call.

XXVIII.

OF MOSES AND HIS WIFE.

HIS Moſes was a fair and comely man;
His wife a swarthy Æthiopian:
Nor did his milk-white boſom change her skin,
She came out thence as black as she went in.
Now Moſes was a type of Moſes' law,
His wife likewiſe of one that never saw
Another way unto eternal life;
There's myſt'ry, then, in Moſes and his wife.

The law is very holy, juſt, and good,
And to it is eſpouſed all fleſh and blood:

But yet the law its goodnefs can't beftow
On any that are wedded thereunto.

Therefore as Mofes' wife came swarthy in,
And went out from him without change of skin :
So he that doth the law for life adore,
Shall yet by it be left a black-a-moor.

XXIX.

OF THE ROSE-BUSH.

THIS homely bush doth to mine eyes expose
A very fair, yea, comely, ruddy rose.
This rose doth always bow its head to me,
Saying, Come, pluck me, I thy rose will be;
Yet offer I to gather rose or bud,
Ten to one but the bush will have my blood.

This looks like a trepan or a decoy,
To offer, and yet snap, who would enjoy;
Yea, the more eager on't, the more in danger,
Be he the master of it or a stranger.

Bush, why doſt bear a roſe if none muſt have it?
Why doſt expoſe it, yet claw thoſe that crave it?
Art become freakiſh? Doſt the wanton play,
Or doth thy teſty humour tend this way?

COMPARISON.

This roſe God's Son is, with His ruddy looks:
But what's the buſh? whoſe pricks, like tenter-hooks,
Do scratch and claw the fineſt lady's hands,
Or rend her clothes, if she too near it stands.

This buſh an emblem is of Adam's race,
Of which Chriſt came, when He His Father's grace
Commended to us in His crimſon blood,
While He in sinners' stead and nature stood.

Thus Adam's race did bear this dainty rose,
And doth the same to Adam's race expoſe.
But thoſe of Adam's race which at it catch,
Them will the race of Adam claw and scratch.

XXX.

OF THE GOING DOWN OF THE SUN.

HAT, haſt thou run thy race, art going down?
Why, as one angry, doſt thou on us frown?
Why wrap thy head with clouds, and hide thy face,
As threat'ning to withdraw from us thy grace?

Oh, leave us not! when once thou hidſt thy head,
Our horizon with darkneſs will be spread.
Tell, who hath thee offended, turn again:
Alas! too late, entreaties are in vain!

COMPARISON.

The gofpel here has had a summer's day,
But in its sunfhine we, like fools, did play;
Or elfe fall out, and with each other wrangle,
And did, inftead of work, not much but jangle.

And if our sun seems angry, hides his face,
Shall it go down, shall night poffefs this place?
Let not the voice of night-birds us afflict,
And of our mif-fpent summer us convict.

XXXI.

UPON THE FROG.

THE frog by nature is both damp and cold,
  Her mouth is large, her belly much will hold;
  She sits somewhat afcending, loves to be
Croaking in gardens, though unpleafantly.

COMPARISON.

The hypocrite is like unto this Frog;
As like as is the puppy to the dog.

He is of nature cold, his mouth is wide
To prate, and at true goodnefs to deride.
And though the world is that which has his love,
He mounts his head, as if he lived above.
And though he seeks in churches for to croak,
He neither seeketh Jefus nor His yoke.

FOR YOUTH.

XXXII.

UPON THE WHIPPING OF A TOP.

IS with the whip the boy sets up the top,
    The whip does make it whirl upon its toe;
Hither and thither makes it skip and hop:
    'Tis with the whip the top is made to go.

COMPARISON.

Our legalift is like this nimble top,
    Without a whip he will not duty do.
Let Mofes whip him, he will skip and hop;
    Forbear to whip, he'll neither stand nor go.

XXXIII.

UPON THE PISMIRE.

MUST we upon the Pismire go to school,
    To learn of her in summer to provide
    For winter next ensuing; man's a fool,
Or silly ants would not be made his guide.
But, sluggard, is it not a shame for thee
    To be outdone by pifmires? Pr'ythee, hear:
Their works, too, will thy condemnation be,
    When at the judgment-seat thou shalt appear.
But since thy God doth bid thee to her go,
    Obey, her ways consider, and be wife:
The Pifmires will inform thee what to do,
    And set the way to life before thine eyes.

FOR YOUTH.

XXXIV.

UPON THE BEGGAR.

HE wants, he asks, he pleads his poverty,
   They within doors do him an alms deny.
   He doth repeat and aggravate his grief;
But they repulſe him, give him no relief.

He begs, they say, Begone: he will not hear,
He coughs and sighs, to shew he still is there;
They disregard him, he repeats his groans;
They still say nay, and he himself bemoans.
They call him vagrant, and more rugged grow;
He cries the shriller; trumpets out his woe.

At laft, when they perceive he 'll take no nay,
An alms they give him without more delay.

COMPARISON.

The beggar doth resemble them that pray
To God for mercy, and will take no nay:
But wait, and count that all his hard gainfays
Are nothing elfe but fatherly delays:
Then imitate him, praying souls, and cry,
There 's nothing like to importunity.

XXXV.

UPON THE HORSE AND HIS RIDER.

HERE'S one rides very sagely on the road:
Shewing that he affects the graveft mode:
Another rides tantivy, or full trot,
To shew such gravity he matters not.

Lo! here comes one amain, he rides full speed,
Hedge, ditch, or miry bog, he doth not heed.
One claws it up-hill, without stop or check,
Another down, as if he'd break his neck.
Now every horse has his efpecial guider:
Then by his going you may know the rider.

COMPARISON.

Now let us turn our horſe into the man,
The rider to a spirit, if we can:
Then let us, by the methods of the guider,
Tell every horſe how he should know his rider.

Some go as men direct, in a right way,
Nor are they suffer'd e'er to go aſtray:
As with a bridle they are govern'd well,
And so are kept from paths that lead to hell.

Now this good man has his eſpecial guider:
Then by his going, let him know his rider.

Another goes as if he did not care,
Whether of heaven or hell he should be heir.
The rein, it seems, is laid upon his neck,
And he pursues his way without a check.

Now this man, too, has his eſpecial guider,
And by his going he may know his rider.

Again, some run as if reſolved to die,
Body and soul to all eternity.
Good counſel they by no means can abide;
They'll have their courſe, whatever them betide.

Now thefe poor men have their efpecial guider,
Were they not fools, they soon might know their rider.

There's one makes head againft all godlinefs,
Thofe, too, that do profefs it he'll diftrefs:
He'll taunt and flout if goodnefs doth appear;
And thofe that love it he will mock and jeer.

Now this man, too, has his efpecial guider;
And by his going he may know his rider.

XXXVI.

UPON THE SIGHT OF A POUND OF CANDLES FALLING TO THE GROUND.

UT are the candles down, and scatter'd too,
   Some lying here, some there? What shall we
     do?
Hold, light the candle there that stands on high,
The other candles you may find thereby.
Light that, I say, and so take up the pound
Which you let fall, and scatter'd on the ground.

COMPARISON.

The fallen candles to us intimate
The bulk of God's elect in their lapfed state;
Their lying scatter'd in the dark may be,
To shew by man's lapfed state his mifery.

The candle that was taken down and lighted,
Thereby to find them fallen and benighted,
Is Jefus Chrift: God by His light doth gather
Whom He will save, and be to them a Father.

XXXVII.

UPON A PENNY LOAF.

THY price one penny is in time of plenty;
In famine doubled 'tis from one to twenty.
Yea, no man knows what price on thee to set,
When there is but one penny loaf to get.

COMPARISON.

The loaf's an emblem of the Word of God,
A thing of low efteem; before the rod
Of famine smites the soul with fear of death:
But then it is our all, our life, our breath.

XXXVIII.

THE BOY AND WATCHMAKER.

THIS watch my father did on me beſtow,
A golden one it is, but 'twill not go,
Unleſs it be at an uncertainty :
But as good none as one to tell a lie.

When 'tis high day, my hand will stand at nine :
I think there's no man's watch so bad as mine.
Sometimes 'tis sullen, 'twill not go at all,
And yet 'twas never broke, nor had a fall.

WATCHMAKER

Your watch, though it be good, through want of skill
May fail to do according to your will.
Suppofe the balance-wheels and spring be good,
And all things elfe, unlefs you underftood
To manage it, as watches ought to be,
Your watch will still be at uncertainty.
Come, tell me, do you keep it from the duft,
And wind it daily, that it may not ruft?
Take heed, too, that you do not strain the spring;
You muft be circumspect in everything,
Or elfe your watch will not exactly go,
'Twill stand, or run too faft, or move too slow.

COMPARISON.

This boy refembles one that's turn'd from sin;
His watch the curious work of grace within.
The Watchmaker is Jefus Chrift our Lord,
His counfel the directions of His Word;
Then, Convert, if thy heart be out of frame,
Of this Watchmaker learn to mend the frame.
Do not lay ope' thy heart to worldly duft,
Nor let thy graces overgrow with ruft;
But oft renew'd in th' spirit of thy mind,
Or elfe uncertain thou thy watch wilt find.

XXXIX.

UPON A LOOKING-GLASS.

IN this, see thou thy beauty, haft thou any;
  Or thy defects, should they be few or many.
  Thou mayft, too, here thy spots and freckles see,
Haft thou but eyes, and what their numbers be.
But art thou blind? There is no looking-glafs
Can shew thee thy defects, thy spots, or face.

COMPARISON.

Unto this glafs we may compare the Word,
For that to man affiftance doth afford.

Has he a mind to know himſelf and state,
To see what will be his eternal fate.

But without eyes, alas! how can he see?
Many that seem to look here, blind men be.
This is the reaſon they so often read
Their judgment there, and do it nothing dread.

XL.

OF THE LOVE OF CHRIST.

THE love of Chrift, poor I! may touch upon;
But 'tis unsearchable. Oh! there is none
Its large dimenfions can comprehend,
Should they dilate thereon, world without end.

When we had sinn'd, He in His zeal did swear,
That He upon His back our sins would bear.
And since to sin there is entailed death,
He vow'd that for our sins He'd lofe His breath.

He did not only say, vow, or refolve,
But to aftonifhment did so involve

Himſelf in man's diſtreſs and miſery,
As for and with him both to live and die.

To His eternal fame in sacred story,
We find that He did lay aſide His glory,
Stepp'd from the throne of higheſt dignity,
Became poor man, did in a manger lie;
Yea, was beholden upon His for bread,
Had, of His own, not where to lay His head:
Though rich, He did for us become thus poor,
That He might make us rich for evermore.

Yet this was but the leaſt of what He did;
But the outſide of what He suffered.
God made His bleſſed Son under the law;
Under the curſe, which, like the lion's paw,
Did rend and tear His soul, for mankind's sin,
More than if we for it in hell had been.
His cries, His tears, and bloody agony,
The nature of His death doth testify.

Nor did He of conſtraint Himſelf thus give
For sin to death, that man might with Him live.
He did do what He did moſt willingly,
He sung, and gave God thanks that He muſt die.
Did ever king die for a captive slave?
Yet such were we whom Jeſus died to save.
Yea, when He made Himſelf a sacrifice,
It was that He might save His enemies.

And, though He was provoked to retract
His bleſt refolves to do so kind an act,
By the abufive carriages of thofe
That did both Him, His love, and grace oppofe ;
Yet He, as unconcern'd about such things,
Goes on, determines to make captive kings :
Yea, many of His murderers He takes
Into His favour, and them princes makes.

XLI.

ON THE CACKLING OF A HEN.

THE Hen so soon as she an egg doth lay,
(Spreads the fame of her doing what she may,)
About the yard a cackling she doth go,
To tell what 'twas she at her neſt did do.

Juſt thus it is with some profeſſing men,
If they do aught that 's good; they, like our hen,
Cannot but cackle on 't where'er they go,
And what their right hand doth their left muſt know.

XLII.

UPON AN HOUR-GLASS.

THIS glafs when made, was by the workman's skill,
The sum of sixty minutes to fulfil.
Time, more nor lefs, by it will out be spun,
But juft an hour, and then the glafs is run.

Man's life we will compare unto this glafs,
The number of his months he cannot pafs :
But when he has accomplished his day,
He, like a vapour, vanifheth away.

XLIII.

UPON A SNAIL.

HE goes but softly, but she goeth sure,
    She stumbles not, as stronger creatures do;
Her journey's shorter, so she may endure
  Better than they which do much further go.

She makes no noife, but stilly seizeth on
  The flower or herb appointed for her food;
The which she quietly doth feed upon,
  While others range and glare, but find no good.

And though she doth but very softly go,
  However slow her pace be, yet 'tis sure;
And certainly they that do travel so,
  The prize which they do aim at they procure.

Although they seem not much to stir or go,
  Who thirſt for Chriſt, and who from wrath do flee;
Yet what they seek for quickly they come too,
  Though it doth seem the furtheſt off to be.

One act of faith doth bring them to that flower
  They so long for, that they may eat and live;
Which to attain is not in other's power,
  Though for it a king's ranſom they would give.

Then let none faint, nor be at all dismay'd,
  That life by Chriſt do seek, they shall not fail
To have it; let them nothing be afraid;
  The herb and flower are eaten by the snail.

XLIV.

OF THE SPOUSE OF CHRIST.

WHO'S this that cometh from the wildernefs,
    Like smoky pillars thus perfumed with myrrh,
    Leaning upon her deareft in diftrefs,
  Placed in His bofom by the Comforter?

She's clothed with the sun, crown'd with twelve stars,
    The spotted moon her footftool she hath made;
The dragon her affaults, fills her with jars,
    Yet refts she under her Beloved's shade.

But whence was she? What is her pedigree?
  Was not her father a poor Amorite?
What was her mother, but as others be,
  A Hittite sinful, poor, and helpless quite.

Yea, as for her, the day that she was born,
  As loathsome, out of doors they did her cast;
Naked and filthy, stinking and forlorn:
  This was her pedigree from first to last.

Nor was she pitied in this estate,
  All let her lie polluted in her blood:
None her condition did commiserate,
  There was no heart that sought to do her good.

Yet she unto these ornaments is come,
  Her breasts are fashion'd, and her hair is grown:
She is made heiress of a heavenly home,
  All her indignities away are blown.

Cast out she was, but now she home is taken,
  Once she was naked, now you see she's clad;
Now made the darling, though before forsaken,
  Bare foot but now as princes' daughters shod.

Instead of filth, she now has her perfumes,
  Instead of ignominy, chains of gold:
Instead of what the beauty most consumes,
  Her beauty's perfect, lovely to behold.

Those that attend and wait upon her be
   Princes of honour clothed in white array;
Upon her head's a crown of gold, and she
   Eats honey, wheat, and oil, from day to day.

For her beloved, He's the high'ſt of all,
   The only Potentate, the King of kings:
Angels and men do Him Jehovah call,
   And from Him life and glory always springs.

He's white and ruddy, and of all the chief;
   His head, His locks, His eyes, His hands, and feet,
Do for completeneſs outdo all belief,
   His cheeks like flowers are, His mouth moſt sweet.

As for His wealth, He is made heir of all,
   What is in heaven, what is in earth is His:
And He this lady His joint heir doth call,
   Of all that shall be, or at preſent is.

Well, lady, well, God has been good to thee;
   Thou of an outcaſt, now art made a queen.
Few or none may with thee compared be,
   A beggar made thus high is seldom seen.

Take heed of pride, remember what thou art
   By nature, though thou haſt in grace a share,
Thou in thyſelf doſt yet retain a part
   Of thine own filthineſs: wherefore beware.

XLV.

UPON A SKILFUL PLAYER ON AN INSTRUMENT.

HE that can play well on an inftrument,
    Will take the ear, and captivate the mind
    With mirth or sadnefs, when it is intent;
And mufic into it a way doth find.

But if one hears that hath therein no skill,
    (As often mufic lights of such a chance,)
Of its brave notes they soon be weary will:
    And there are some can neither sing nor dance.

COMPARISON.

To him that thus moſt skilfully doth play,
  God doth compare a goſpel-miniſter,
That doth with life and vigour preach and pray,
  Applying right what he doth there infer.

Whether this man of wrath or grace doth preach,
  So skilfully he handles every word,
And by his saying, doth the heart so reach,
  That it doth joy or sigh before the Lord.

But some there be, which, as the brute doth lie
  Under the word, without the leaſt advance :
Such do deſpiſe the goſpel miniſtry ;
  They weep not at it, neither to it dance.

XLVI.

OF MAN BY NATURE.

 ROM God he's a backslider,
   Of ways he loves the wider;
   With wickedness a sider,
More venom than a spider.

In sin he's a confider,
A make-bate and divider;
Blind reason is his guider,
The devil is his rider.

XLVII.

UPON THE DISOBEDIENT CHILD.

HILDREN, when little, how do they delight us!
When they grow bigger, they begin to fright us.
Their sinful nature prompts them to rebel,
And to delight in paths that lead to hell.
Their parents' love and care they overlook,
As if relation had them quite forsook.
They take the counsels of the wanton rather
Than the moft grave inftructions of a father.
They reckon parents ought to do for them,
Though they the fifth commandment do contemn.

They snap and snarl, if parents them control,
Although in things moſt hurtful to the soul;
They reckon they are maſters, and that we
Who parents are should to them subject be!
If parents fain would have a hand in chooſing,
The children have a heart still in refuſing.
They, by wrong doings, from their parents gather,
And say it is no sin to rob a father.
They 'll joſtle parents out of place and power,
They 'll make themselves the head, and them devour.
How many children by becoming head
Have brought their parents to a piece of bread!
Thus they who at the firſt were parents' joy,
Turn that to bitterneſs, themſelves deſtroy.

But, wretched child, how canſt thou thus requite
Thy aged parents, for that great delight
They took in thee, when thou as helpleſs lay
In their indulgent boſoms day by day?
Thy mother, long before she brought thee forth,
Took care thou shouldſt want neither food nor cloth.
Thy father glad was at his very heart,
Had he to thee a portion to impart.
Comfort they promiſed themſelves in thee,
But thou, it seems, to them a grief will be.
How oft, how willingly, brake they their sleep,
If thou, their bantling, didſt but wince or weep!
Their love to thee was such, they could have given,
That thou mightſt live, all but their part of heaven.

But now, behold, how they rewarded are!
For their indulgent love and tender care,
All is forgot, this love they do defpife,
They brought this bird up to pick out their eyes.

XLVIII.

UPON A SHEET OF WHITE PAPER.

 HIS paper's handled by the sons of men,
Both with the faireſt and the fouleſt pen.
'Twill alſo shew what is upon it writ,
Whether 'tis wiſely done, or void of wit.
Each blot and blur it alſo will expoſe
To the next readers, be they friends or foes.

COMPARISON.

Some souls are like unto this blank or sheet,
(Though not in whiteneſs:) The next man they meet,

Be what he will, a good man or deluder,
A knave or fool, the dangerous intruder
May write thereon, to caufe that man to err,
In doctrine or in life, with blot and blur.
Nor will that soul conceal wherein it swerves,
But shew itfelf to each one that obferves.
A reading man may know who was the writer,
And by the hellifh nonfenfe the inditer.

XLIX.

UPON THE FIRE.

WHO falls into the fire shall burn with heat,
While thofe remote scorn from it to retreat.
Yea, while thofe in it cry out, "Oh! I burn,"
Some further off thofe cries to laughter turn.

COMPARISON.

While some tormented are in hell for sin,
On earth some greatly do delight therein.
Yea, while some make it echo with their cry,
Others count it a fable and a lie.

www.ingramcontent.com/pod-product-compliance
Lightning Source LLC
Chambersburg PA
CBHW020124170426
43199CB00009B/627